the little book of

Bourbon

the spirit of America

Eric Zandona

my wife Tia

First published in Great Britain in 2023 by Mitchell Beazley, an imprint of Octopus Publishing Group Ltd
Carmelite House
50 Victoria Embankment
London EC4Y 0DZ
www.octopusbooks.co.uk

An Hachette UK Company
www.hachette.co.uk
www.octopusbooksusa.com

Text copyright
© Eric Zandona 2018
Design and layout copyright
© Octopus Publishing Group 2018

Distributed in the US by
Hachette Book Group
1290 Avenue of the Americas
4th and 5th Floors, New York, NY 10104

Distributed in Canada by
Canadian Manda Group
664 Annette St, Toronto, Ontario, Canada M6S 2C8

ISBN 978-1-7847-2911-0

A CIP catalogue record for this book is available from the British Library.

Printed and bound in China

10 9 8 7 6 5 4 3 2 1

Publisher Lucy Pessell
Designer Isobel Platt
Editor Feyi Oyesanya
Assistant Editor Samina Rahman
Production Controller Nic Jones and Lucy Carter

All gallons stated are US gallons

Page 2: Founded by Lincoln Henderson, former Master Distiller of Brown-Forman, Angel's Envy Distillery opened in 2016 and began producing bourbon and rye whiskey to supplement and eventually replace their purchased whiskey.

Bourbon

A quick history

Since the beginning of the 21st century, bourbon has been on a steady climb in popularity with countries such as Japan, Australia, Germany and the United Kingdom all developing a taste for bourbon like never before.

But to the uninitiated, the world of bourbon can be a daunting place, with a wealth of unfamiliar terms and techniques. The Little Book of Bourbon aims to help the novice bourbon fan navigate that world, providing an introduction to the history, production and flavours of bourbon for those who are just discovering America's native spirit.

The opening section – The Basics – offers the reader a solid foundation for understanding the historical and technical aspects of how bourbon is made and why it tastes the way it does, and decodes the language and terminology found on its labels. The Cocktails offers time-honoured drinks that pair perfectly with bourbon and bring out the very best in this wonderful spirit.

Ultimately, through The Little Book of Bourbon, I hope to share my belief that the subjective experience of flavour – not price, popularity or rarity – is the most important reason to drink any particular bourbon. Whatever kind of bourbon you enjoy, use this book to guide you through the wonderful world of flavours that is waiting to be explored.

A QUICK HISTORY OF BOURBON

Much has been written about the history of bourbon whiskey and its place in the wider story of the United States. However, while bourbon is more than 200 years old, the work of fully understanding the part it has played in American history – and where it intersects with the stories of Native Americans, immigrants, women, slaves, politics and religion – has only just begun.

Distilled spirits have had an important economic and social role in the lives of Americans from the time of the British colonies to the present day. Not long after European colonization of the Americas, settlers tasked themselves with using both local and imported crops to make fermented drinks. In 1587, English settlers at Roanoke made beer from corn because it provided a safe source of water and nutrition – and some alcohol. As the colonies grew, beer from barley and cider from apples and pears became more common and widely available. At the same time, distilleries were popping up to produce spirits from locally grown grain and imported molasses. By 1770, New England had 159 rum distilleries, which made the spirit very inexpensive and popular. Rum became an important part of the triangular trade that moved raw materials, finished goods, weapons and slaves between Africa, the Americas and Europe. However, the American

Revolution (1775–83), among other things, made the importation of molasses from the West Indies more expensive so many distillers turned to grain for making whiskey.

Throughout the 18th and 19th centuries American settlers – allowed to claim 160 hectares (400 acres) of land and purchase an additional 400 hectares (1,000 acres) – pushed west into the Appalachian frontier.

On 31 December 1776, the Virginia General Assembly established that the region beyond the Appalachian Mountains should be designated Kentucky County. Later, in 1780, Kentucky County was split into three smaller counties: Jefferson, Lincoln and Fayette. Fayette County was named after the Marquis de Lafayette who fought alongside the Americans in the American Revolution, and in 1785 Bourbon County was carved out of Fayette County and named in honour of the French royal house of Bourbon, who also provided aid during the war. On 1 June 1792, Kentucky was admitted as the 15th state in the Union. Throughout this period, farmers established homesteads and began planting maize, also called Indian corn. Like their eastern predecessors, these farmers distilled their excess crops into whiskey and began selling and bartering with it.

At this point, questions arise. Who thought to purposely age corn whiskey in charred barrels, and

THE WHISKEY REBELLION

While corn and barley were grown throughout the newly formed United States, rye was the most popular grain for farming and for whiskey.

Farmers on the frontier of western Pennsylvania and other states found that it was easier to distil their rye into whiskey and sell or barter with it than attempt to cart it hundreds of miles to the larger population centres. However, in 1791, George Washington passed an excise tax on distilled spirits to help pay off the country's significant debt from the American Revolution. Farm distillers on the frontier, who often lacked cash, resented this and attempted to evade the tax. In 1794, a revolt broke out when US Marshals attempted to enforce payment of the tax. The home of tax inspector John Neville was burned down and in response President George Washington called up 13,000 militiamen and rode into Pennsylvania to squash the so-called Whiskey Rebellion. This was an important turning point in the history of the United States, demonstrating the power of the Federal government and its willingness to enforce its laws. The excise tax remained in effect until 1802 when Thomas Jefferson took office as the third president of the United States.

when did this happen? And why was it called bourbon? The truth is, there is no definitive historical evidence that answers these questions. The first printed reference to bourbon whiskey comes from an 1821 advertisement in Bourbon County, and the first written association of bourbon with charred barrels came in 1826 when a Lexington grocer requested whiskey stored in "burnt" barrels. However, these references only point to the fact that by the 1820s it was already well established that there was a whiskey coming out of Kentucky known as bourbon, famed for being stored in charred barrels.

Without direct evidence of when and who first stored corn whiskey in charred barrels and called it bourbon, historians have tried to piece together the most plausible answers. The most repeated – and probably incorrect – answer given is that Elijah Craig, a Baptist minister, invented bourbon in 1789. While Craig was a distiller, among other things, there is no indication that his whiskey was any different from his neighbours' and the first reference to his invention of bourbon does not materialize until 1874.

What seems more likely is that there was no single inventor of bourbon, but many. It is certain that in the late 18th century almost all farmers produced some amount of whiskey from their excess grain. Barrels were the most common medium in which to ship goods, and it was also a common practice to recycle barrels. If one wanted to reuse a barrel without absorbing the odours and flavours of the previous contents, it was known that you could simply char the inside to neutralize the barrel. Given these historical facts it seems likely that multiple farmers distilled a mash of corn and other grains and put the resulting whiskey into barrels they had charred to remove previous flavours. When these whiskeys were sold down the river, it was probably noticeable that the spirit from charred barrels had a unique and particularly pleasant flavour compared to whiskey matured in raw or toasted barrels. As a result, it is likely that demand for this type of whiskey grew. Without more historical research, we cannot know for certain if bourbon whiskey was named after the county or the famous New Orleans Street, but at present it seems more likely it was referencing the county, especially since the first printed reference to it comes from Bourbon County, Kentucky, and not New Orleans.

The 19th Century
Throughout the first half of the 19th century, bourbon steadily grew in popularity and distribution, in part because of several improvements to the fermentation process that helped maintain quality. In 1818, the first recorded reference to a distiller using what's known as

the sour mash process appears. Catherine Carpenter of Casey County, Kentucky, put a portion of a fully fermented batch of mash back into a fresh mash to begin fermentation. Whether she or other distillers at the time knew why this worked is unclear but the result was fewer spoiled fermentations, and improved quality and consistency in flavour and attenuation (the ability of yeast to convert all the available sugar to alcohol).

By the 1850s the process of making bourbon had significantly improved, in no small part due to the work of Dr James C. Crow, for whom Old Crow Bourbon is named. Born in Inverness, Scotland, Crow studied chemistry and medicine at the University of Edinburgh before moving to Kentucky in the 1820s. In 1835, Dr Crow was working at the Glenns Creek Distillery in Woodford County, Kentucky, and began refining the sour mash process and using his training to better understand the process of making bourbon, why certain practices worked and how to improve the flavour and quality of his bourbon through science. As a result of this work, Dr Crow helped to create what we know as bourbon today.

By 1865, the American Civil War had curtailed most commercial production of bourbon and slowed its growth. (This pattern would be repeated during World War I and World War II.) After the war, distillers set up shop once again and began producing bourbon. In this post-war period, most bourbon was sold by the barrel and drinkers who did not make their own would buy bourbon at a bar or from a grocer. At a bar, barrels were tapped and the bourbon served to customers; at the grocery, people would bring their own jugs or containers and take the bourbon home. During this period, the practice of diluting the bourbon to make each barrel go further and increase profits was widespread.

Middlemen known as rectifiers would buy aged bourbon by the barrel from distilleries and then dilute the bourbon with water. The barrels of this cut bourbon were sold to bars and grocers, who in turn would water down the bourbon again.

By this point the whiskey was so diluted that it had lost a significant amount of its colour, flavour and alcohol. To counteract this, people added neutral alcohol, prune juice or even acid to make the "whiskey" seem more like the real thing. It was also at this time that rectifiers began "inventing" new technologies for rapidly ageing whiskey. In reality, many of these companies were creating imitation whiskey by combining inexpensive neutral spirit, acids, fruit juices, iodine, tobacco and wood extracts to sell as bourbon or other types of whiskey. Not surprisingly, bourbon distillers were unhappy about this bastardization of their whiskey and imitation products sold on the coat-tails of their hard work.

MOUNT VERNON DISTILLERY

In 1797, after serving two terms as president, George Washington returned home to Virginia and, at the prompting of Scottish farm manager James Anderson, built a distillery at Mount Vernon to make whiskey from some of his excess grain. Anderson and six slaves made brandy and whiskey distilled from a mash of 60% rye, 35% corn and 5% barley. His common whiskey was distilled twice and sold for 50 cents per gallon (about 13 cents per litre) and a more expensive special whiskey was distilled four times and sold for $1 per gallon (about 26 cents per litre). In 1799, Washington sold 10,500 gallons (39,750 litres) of whiskey, making him the largest and most profitable distiller in Virginia. However, this success was short-lived, coming to an end when the distillery was closed after Washington's death in December 1799.

The Bottled-In-Bond Act

In response, a number of distillers led by Colonel Edmund Haynes Taylor, Jr worked with the US Secretary of the Treasury, John G. Carlisle, to create the Bottled-in-Bond Act of 1897. During the Civil War, the alcohol excise tax was reinstated but collecting the taxes was easier said than done. The Bottled-in-Bond Act provided benefits for distillers who wanted to protect their products from adulteration, the US Treasury who could collect its excise tax and drinkers who wanted authentic bourbon. Although Old Forester Bourbon was the first branded bourbon to be sold solely in sealed bottles in 1870, until the Bottled-in-Bond Act came into force, it and other distillers had no legal recourse to protect their whiskey from tampering.

The Bottled-in-Bond Act allowed distilleries to create a bonded warehouse that was supervised by an on-site US agent, where whiskey or brandy could mature – tax free. Once the spirit reached four years old, the distiller, in the presence of the agent, could vat barrels of the same type (bourbon, rye, malt etc.) produced in the same season (spring season was defined as January–July; autumn season July–January) and reduce the alcohol strength using pure water to 100 proof (50% ABV). Once the spirit was proofed down, it had to be put in bottles clearly marked with the name of the distillery, when it was distilled and when it was bottled before it was sealed with a federal strip stamp, all inside the bonded warehouse. The stamp meant that distillers only had to pay excise tax on the spirit that was actually bottled and left their warehouses. It also indicated to the buying public the high standard under which the spirit was produced and made it a federal crime to tamper with the bottle or the liquid inside the bottle once it was stamped. This law was a watershed moment – the first-ever US consumer protection law establishing that the government would guarantee the product in the bottle met certain standards and was sold as advertised. Rather unsurprisingly, rectifiers were not happy and immediately challenged the new law in court.

In 1906, Upton Sinclair published The Jungle, which exposed the horrid conditions of the US meat packing industry. In response, public outcry for more transparency and truth in labelling led to the passage of the Pure Food and Drug Act at the end of Theodore Roosevelt's presidency. The law allowed for the labelling of pure whiskey, but there was no written definition of what constituted whiskey. In response to pressure from both rectifiers and distillers, President William Howard Taft decided to settle this dispute. In 1909, after six months of deliberation and input from rectifiers and straight whiskey distillers, President Taft established definitions for straight whiskey, blended whiskey and imitation whiskey. The Taft Decision, as it became

known, created the basic definition of straight bourbon that we use today: a spirit made from a fermented mash of at least 51% corn distilled to less than 160 proof (80% ABV) and barrelled at less than 125 proof (62.5% ABV) in charred oak barrels and aged for two years. However, bourbon distillers were not completely satisfied, because Taft's decision also created legal definitions for the blended and imitation whiskeys the rectifiers were selling.

Temperance

At the end of the 19th and beginning of the 20th centuries, economic and social forces in the United States gradually reduced the number of operating bourbon distilleries. The new national market facilitated by the interstate railway system and mass market advertising led to increasing market pressure for consolidation of the bourbon industry, which offered reduced competition and increased profits. At the same time the temperance movement, which started off with the simple message that Americans should moderate their drinking, gradually shifted to the radical proposal that all production, sale and consumption of alcohol should be completely prohibited.

The temperance movement began for good reason. In 1830, the per capita consumption of pure alcohol was 7.1 gallons (26.9 litres) per year – the equivalent of 53.25

bottles of 40% ABV bourbon per year, or slightly more than one bottle a week for every man, woman and child in the United States. By 1916, the message of temperance had worked, and the per capita consumption of pure alcohol dropped dramatically to 1.96 gallons (7.42 litres) per year. Then, on 6 April 1917, the United States declared war on Germany and entered World War I. With the declaration of war, US industries – including distilleries – shifted production to support the war effort. Instead of making bourbon, patriotic distilleries produced neutral spirits, which were used in munition making.

After the war, conditions for bourbon distillers did not improve a great deal. In 1920, the US Congress ratified the Eighteenth Amendment to the United States Constitution, establishing the national Prohibition of alcohol production, transpiration and sale. Despite the new law, a few distilleries were able to sell their remaining stock of bourbon as "medicinal alcohol" and the Old Fire Copper Distillery (which still operates today as the Buffalo Trace Distillery) was allowed to continue making whiskey for medicinal purposes.

The Great Depression and World War II
By 1933, when the Twenty-first Amendment repealed Prohibition, much of the country's aged whiskey stock was depleted and the country was in the midst of the

Great Depression, making capital for producing and ageing bourbon more difficult to come by. In 1936, Congress passed the Federal Alcohol Administration Act, which created the new legal framework for regulating alcohol production and labelling post-Prohibition. This new law essentially recodified the Taft Decision with one minor change. Without fanfare, the definition of bourbon was amended to include the requirement that the whiskey be aged in new charred oak barrels. The only rationale for this change was that, in the midst of the Great Depression, the requirement to use new barrels for bourbon would essentially create and sustain jobs for coopers. By 1941, the United States was back at war and once again the bourbon industry was called upon to serve its country and produce industrial alcohol for munitions.

By the end of World War II, the economy was booming and things at last started to look up for bourbon producers. Throughout the 1950s and 1960s demand for bourbon grew and distillers responded with large increases in production. In 1964, Congress declared bourbon to be America's Native Spirit. There was, however, an underlying problem. The American palate was undergoing a significant shift in its taste preference for whiskey, in part due to the catalogue of disruptions to bourbon production during the first half of the 20th century. Lighter-style whiskeys such as Canadian Club

were growing in popularity, partly because it was widely available during Prohibition and the Great Depression, but also because of a generational shift. Young drinkers were looking for something new, not their parents' or grandparents' old bourbon. By the mid-1970s the bottom had fallen out of the bourbon market as drinkers flocked to light-flavoured whiskeys and vodka, which left bourbon distillers with a huge glut of ageing barrels.

Modern Times

In the 1980s and 1990s, when bourbon popularity was at its nadir, a few important changes took place. In 1984, the Sazerac Company created Blanton's Single Barrel Bourbon, which was the first modern bourbon ever bottled from one barrel. Then in 1986, Heaven Hill introduced the first "small batch" bourbon, which at the time was made of bourbon aged for a minimum of 12 years. Three years later in 1989, the first bottling of Old Rip Van Winkle 15-year-old bourbon was released. Soon after, Jim Beam followed suit with four new bourbons to create its small batch collection. All of these innovations were possible because the bourbon industry had slow sales and was sitting on millions of barrels that were only getting older.

By the early 2000s, tastes slowly began to change again. A renewed interest in classic cocktails and the emergence of the craft distilling movement helped to drive more interest in brown spirits in general and bourbon in particular. This rediscovery of bourbon by a new generation of drinkers has continued to grow and today there are more barrels of bourbon ageing in Kentucky than there are people in the state.

Interestingly, this bourbon boom occurred so suddenly that a number of bourbons had to drop their age statements or have become very difficult to find due to huge demand. Thankfully, there are still hundreds of bourbon, straight bourbon and bottled-in-bond bourbon brands on the market at all price points and flavour profiles. So, while it may be difficult to find that one particular bottle, there are many great brands worth trying.

While the history of bourbon reveals that the good times never last, there also seems to be little slowdown in consumer demand for high-quality bourbon whiskey. So now is the time to go out and get a bottle, or order a glass at your favourite bar, and enjoy one of the world's truly great whiskeys.

Bourbon

How it's made

A dictionary definition of bourbon would read something like "A whiskey distilled from a mash consisting of a minimum of 51% corn." While this definition is true, it misses some of the key components of how bourbon is made. These components are not only necessary to meet the carefully protected legal definition created by US Congress, but they also provide information about why bourbon tastes the way it does. Grain selection, water, yeast, fermentation, distillation, maturation, vatting, filtration and proofing all play a role in shaping the flavour profile of each bourbon and inform our experience of drinking and hopefully enjoying it.

The key ingredients

All bourbons begin with the creation of what's known as a mash bill – the selection of particular grains and their ratios that form the backbone of the flavour profile. The only legal mandate for bourbon with respect to its mash is that it must contain at least 51% corn; malted barley, rye and wheat are the other most commonly used grains.

Corn

Corn is, of course, the defining grain for bourbon and typically accounts for 70–80% of the mash bill, sometimes less. It contributes a sense of sweetness to the final drink, although standard yellow corn can lose many of its other flavour characteristics after ageing in wooden barrels. Most distillers use the standard No. 2 yellow dent corn because of its availability and high starch content, but a few craft distillers have begun using heirloom varieties of white, blue, red and yellow corn in their bourbons. These heirloom varieties offer great flavours for small batch operations – you are not likely to see them used in any of the big Kentucky bourbons any time soon as there is simply not enough being grown and they tend to have lower yields.

+ Rye and/or Wheat

Rye and wheat are known as flavouring grains, since the taste they impart stays intact over the ageing process. They can account for as little as 8% to as much as 35% of the mash. Rye, the most common flavouring grain, adds dryness and a spicy character to bourbon, which harmonizes beautifully with the sweetness that comes from the corn and the vanilla notes extracted from the barrel.

Wheat is the next most common flavouring grain used in bourbon and it is traditionally described as being somewhat sweeter, adding softness and a slight nutty character. This perception of sweetness comes from the fact that wheat does not have the same dryness and spice of rye, so it allows more of the bourbon's natural sweetness to come through. Wheated bourbons are not

necessarily softer or sweeter, but rather wheat allows more of the flavour choices made in the distillation, barrelling and proofing processes to come to the fore.

+ Malted Barley

Malted barley usually makes up about 5–10% of the mash but plays a significant role, providing all of the enzymes necessary to convert the grains' starch into the simple sugars required to make alcohol. Barley often contributes biscuit and nutty flavours to bourbon, characteristics similar to those you might find in a single malt Scotch whisky.

+ Water

For good reason one of the main talking points of making bourbon is the water. It can account for up to 60% of what is in the bottle and it plays an important role in fermentation. In Kentucky, they like to brag that their limestone-filtered water is perfect for making bourbon. This claim has a good basis in reality, as water that has worked its way through limestone tends to be low in iron and higher in other minerals. Yeast struggles in high-iron environments and becomes less capable of fermenting sugars into alcohol.

Similarly, other minerals serve as micronutrients to the yeast and help keep them happy and healthy longer into the fermentation process. Water with the right pH will also help the yeast outcompete other microorganisms that might otherwise spoil the mash.

Skipping ahead briefly, good water plays an important role in proofing the spirit down from cask to bottling strength, as water with a high mineral content can cause salts and minerals to solidify and collect on the bottom of the bottle. Alternatively, water with almost no mineral content affects the aroma and mouthfeel of the spirit. So the right type of water is very important.

Bourbon Is Born

Cooking
Once a mash bill has been selected, the grains are milled, mixed with water and cooked, breaking down the proteins in the grains and gelatinizing the starch. After the starch is gelatinized, the enzymes in the malted barley begin to break down the starch molecules in the mash bill into fermentable sugars. The process to this point is similar to the mashing process in beer making, and in an efficient distillery, can take as little as an hour to complete.

▼ Sour mash process
Next, the cooked mash is cooled down and pumped to the fermentation tank. This can vary from closed stainless steel tanks to rustic open tanks made from

Major and minor mash bills

There are three major mash bills (rye, high-rye and wheated) used in most Kentucky bourbons and Tennessee whiskeys, as well as a further two minor mash bills (four-grain and non-typical) that are less common but in use among some craft distillers. Of the three major bourbon bills, the rye mash bill is the most commonly used and consists of about 75–80% corn, 10–15% rye and 5–10% malted barley. The high-rye mash bill increases the rye content, shifting the balance to about 55–77% corn, 18–35% rye and 5–10% malted barley. The wheated mash bill replaces rye entirely and instead uses wheat, commonly at a ratio of about 70–81% corn, 14–20% wheat and 5–10% malted barley. The two lesser-used mash bills offer a little more flexibility for craft distillers to experiment with. The four-grain mash bill is a combination of corn, rye, wheat and malted barley, but since this is less common it is difficult to give approximate ratios. Lastly, the non-typical mash bill refers to any mash that includes secondary grains other than rye or wheat. Some distillers have included oats, millet, quinoa, triticale, spelt and even brown rice in their bourbon mashes and each adds unique flavours and characteristics to the mouthfeel of the final product.

cypress wood, or anything in between. The mash needs to be cooled to about 21°C (70°F), at which point the sour mash process takes place. Previously fermented mash (sometimes called backset) and/or spent beer – the leftover liquid from the still after all the alcohol has been stripped out – is added to a new ferment at this stage. Both backset and spent beer have a low pH and taste sour. And, as Dr Crow demonstrated, lowering the pH of the new mash helps the yeast propagate quickly to outcompete other microorganisms, giving higher yields.

▼ **Distillation**

Distillation is the process of separating various chemical compounds based on boiling points. Because alcohol boils at 78.4°C (173°F) and water boils at 100°C (212°F), slowly heating a mixture will cause the alcohol to evaporate first, leaving behind most of the water. This simple idea has been practiced for millennia around the world. However, it wasn't until the 8th century ad that the scientist Abu Mūsā Jābir ibn Hayyān, sometimes referred to as "the father of chemistry", made a major technological advance in distilling with the creation of the alembic pot still. This was so effective that pot stills based on this design are still being used.

The last major advancement in distilling technology occurred in 1830 when Aeneas Coffey, an Irish excise tax collector, was granted a patent for two column stills in series that could be operated continuously. The Coffey still, as it became known, was highly efficient, could produce spirits that were much cleaner and smoother than those made in other stills of its time and could be fed non-stop. Coffey's design ideas for the continuous column still became so popular they remain in use today and are used to make most bourbon, Canadian whisky and Scottish grain whisky.

At almost all large Kentucky bourbon distilleries, fully fermented mash is pumped from the fermentation tank to the beer still (a very large column filled with perforated plates). The beer, grist and all, is pumped in near the top of the still while large amounts of steam are pumped in from the bottom. As the beer and steam meet, the heat causes the alcohol and other volatile compounds to boil and rise toward the top of the still. As these vapours rise, they recondense on perforated plates inside the still and revaporize as they are hit with more steam. This process of boiling, condensing and reboiling is repeated again and again throughout the entire height of the still, causing alcohol vapours to concentrate at the top while the majority of the water and all of the solids fall to the bottom, to be pumped out as spent beer.

After leaving the beer still, the alcohol vapours pass through a second vessel known as a doubler. The doubler is filled with an alcohol solution called "low wines", which is usually somewhere in the 30% ABV range. As the alcohol vapours pass through the doubler it further concentrates the alcohol, and the resulting distillate – sometimes referred to as "white dog" – comes off the still at about 69–70% ABV.

In addition to alcohol and flavour compounds, there are a number of potentially harmful compounds which must be removed from the distillate. Acetone, methanol, butanol and more – a natural part of the organic chemistry that occurs during fermentation – are known to be dangerous in concentrated amounts. The distiller must take great care to separate out as much of these potentially harmful compounds as possible, while collecting the majority of the alcohol and the flavour and aromatic compounds that give the drink its pleasant taste.

In a modern column still, the processes of feeding the still, concentrating the alcohol, separating out the harmful compounds and removing the spent beer all happen simultaneously. However, in a pot still, which is more commonly used among craft distillers, each of these steps is more distinct and easily observed. Since pot stills are less efficient, it typically takes two runs to make a single batch of distillate that will go into a barrel.

▼ **The stripping run**

The aim of the first run, called the stripping run, is to simply concentrate the alcohol as much as possible from the solids and some of the water. The still is "charged" with beer and the distiller begins heating the still, either by using a steam jacket around the outside of the still or an old-fashioned direct flame. Either way, the contents of the still need to be stirred constantly to prevent any of the solids from burning and tainting the batch with unpleasant flavours. During the stripping run, the low wines that come off the still are collected and saved for the second spirit run.

▼ **The spirit run**

During the spirit run the distiller has to make some very important choices on when to make his or her cuts. As the still heats up to about 56°C (132.8°F), acetone begins to boil and vaporize, followed by methanol at 64.7°C (148.5°F). As these vapours rise to the top of the pot, they come to a junction called the lyne arm, which connects the pot to the condenser. Once the vapours enter the condenser, a cold liquid circulates around the pipe carrying them. As the vapours cool, they recondense and come out of the still as a liquid. Since this first liquid off the still, called the "heads", contains a variety of hazardous chemicals, it is collected in a special container and is either discarded or occasionally used to clean the floors. After the heads have been "cut", and the distiller notices that the unpleasant solvent notes have disappeared, what's known as the "hearts" will start to be collected. Made up of pleasant flavour and aromatic compounds, alcohol and some heavier fusel alcohols – this will eventually become the bourbon you find in the bottle. As the hearts cut nears its end, the spirit coming from the still will taste very hot and harsh, even though the alcohol content is decreasing. When making a white spirit, such as vodka, gin, unaged brandy or rum, the aim is to cut out all of the fusel alcohols because they are unpleasant to drink.

However, when producing a spirit to age, the distiller wants to leave some amount of fusel alcohols in the hearts cut because they will eventually oxidize and add more character and complexity to the spirit over time. Once the flavour shifts away from the pleasant characteristics the distiller is looking for, the hearts will stop being collected and the "tails" cut will be made. The tails consist of ethanol, fusel alcohols and a number of heavier aroma and flavour compounds that are typically unpleasant. Some distillers turn the still off at this point, while others keep it running and recycle some of the tails into the next stripping run to get a little extra alcohol out of the next batch.

Ageing and Barrelling

Ultimately, when making bourbon, a recipe is not crafted for what it will taste like coming off the still, but rather how it will taste coming out of the barrel. It takes a little imagination and a lot of practical experience not to distil for today but for four, six, eight, even twenty years in the future.

Unlike the laws for Scotch whisky, which require both a minimum number of years in wood and a maximum barrel size, bourbon's definition does not specify a length of time or a barrel size. However, in practice almost all bourbon is aged in 200 litre (53 gallon) barrels made from charred new American white oak (Quercus alba) for at least four years. It is easy to think of the maturation phase as a period of inactivity, but that would be far from the truth.

Oak

Before the barrel is made, tall oak trees from the Ozark Mountains are logged, split and cut into staves. The most prized barrels come from "yard-seasoned" staves, which have been stacked outside and left to the elements. Oak is mostly made of cellulose, which gives the wood its structural integrity and allows the barrel to be watertight – but being watertight also means the whiskey cannot interact much with the wood, which is why seasoning is so important. The heat, cold, rain, humidity and sunlight cause mould and other microorganisms to grow on the wood staves as they sit for 12–36 months out in the yard. During this time the wood degrades slightly, developing very tiny fractures, which allow the bourbon to penetrate deeper into the wood, picking up some of its characteristics and infusing the end drink with flavour.

▼ Charring

Once the wood is fully seasoned, it is taken to the cooper, who fashions it by hand into a barrel. The finished barrel (minus the end caps) is then placed over a small fire and the interior is allowed to burn. The resulting char creates a layer of charcoal that acts like a filter as the whiskey is pushed in and out of the wood by seasonal cycles of cold and hot temperatures. How long the fire burns determines how deeply the layer of char penetrates the barrel, and this length of time is measured in numbers: for a No. 1 char, the fire lasts for 15 seconds; No. 2 char lasts for 30 seconds; No. 3 char for 35 seconds; and the No. 4 – or alligator – char for 55 seconds. Char numbers 3 and 4 are the most commonly found, but the different timescales involved offer more adventurous distillers' room to experiment. Buffalo Trace Distillery once released a handful of identical bourbons with differing levels of char, going all the way to No. 7.

▼ Ageing

As the bourbon sits ageing in the barrels, the flavour compounds from fermentation that have been concentrated in the still begin to interact and mix with the char and the oak compounds extracted by the alcohol. In addition to this, oxygen is able to pass through the wood and react with the spirit as the barrel sits in the warehouse. This process of oxidation slowly breaks down some of the harsher fusel alcohols into smaller components that add body and greater complexity to the end product.

This intricate process of maturation is complicated by the fact that small changes in a barrel's temperature or the average humidity in the surrounding air can significantly affect the flavour of the bourbon inside. Generally, barrels that sit on the top floors of a rickhouse – a special warehouse used to store bourbon barrels – are spicier, more intense and have more oak flavours, whereas the barrels on the slightly cooler, more humid lower floors have a softer character with less intensity. Because no two barrels are the same, producers will usually take multiple barrels, from different parts of the rickhouse, and mix them to build the desired flavour profile.

▼ Vatting

This process of mixing barrels is known as vatting or blending. Blending is sometimes looked down on in the bourbon world because, according to US government guidelines, blended whiskey is a category of spirits allowed to contain a mixture of 20% whiskey and up to 80% "neutral spirit" (high strength vodka). Despite this negative association, the ability of a master blender to create a consistent flavour profile again and again from different barrels is a tremendous skill.

▼ Filtering

Once vatted, producers make the decision whether or not to filter the bourbon. Some producers choose not to filter their bourbon because they believe it can negatively affect its flavour. Others may charcoal filter – a process that primarily removes any small residual particulate from the barrel and polishes the look of the spirit – or chill filter their bourbon. Chill filtering is a process in which the whiskey is quickly cooled to between -10°C (14°F) and 4°C (39°F) and then pushed through a filter. Chilling the whiskey causes fatty acid chains to make the spirit cloudy. As the bourbon is filtered, the fatty acids are removed, producing a clearer liquid. The fatty acids are not necessarily harmful, but some producers choose to protect the visual appeal of the bourbon especially in areas with very cold winters.

Some critics of chill filtration believe that these fatty acids positively contribute to the flavour and body of the whiskey and that keeping them is worth any potential cloudiness.

▼ Proofing

Finally, the last step in the process before bottling is to reduce the alcohol content of the bourbon from cask strength to bottling strength. If the bourbon is at 62% ABV after being vatted and filtered, and the target strength is 45% ABV, pure water is gradually added to the bourbon until the target strength is reached. This needs to be done slowly, because if water is added too quickly it can cause a chemical reaction which gives the spirit a faint aroma of liquid soap. Once the water is added, the bourbon is allowed to rest so that the alcohol and water fully integrate.

When rested, the bourbon is ready to be bottled, labelled and shipped, ultimately to be opened and enjoyed at your local bar or at home.

Bourbon

Cocktails

Bourbon is a wonderful spirit that is hugely versatile. While many bourbon enthusiasts love to drink their whiskey neat, on the rocks or with a few drops of water, bourbon also does a fantastic job in hundreds of classic and contemporary cocktails.

Here I've pulled together 20 classic, time-honoured bourbon cocktails that offer a range of takes on the basic bourbon flavour profile, and run the gamut from tall and light to dark and complex. While almost any variety of bourbon can be used for each of these cocktails, you will find that you develop your own preferences as you drink them – the experimentation is all part of the enjoyment.

A number of the recipes use a Simple Sugar Syrup:

Heat one part sugar and one part water in a small pan and stir until the sugar is completely dissolved. Ensure that it heats to at least 60°C/140°F (a simmer).

Cool and store in a sterilized bottle or jar in the refrigerator for up to 2 weeks.

In my experience, there is no correlation between the cost of a bourbon and the quality of the cocktail. Good vermouth, freshly squeezed juices and fresh garnishes will pay greater dividends than splurging for a high-end bourbon and cutting corners in other places.

Boulevardier

The Boulevardier was created by Erskine Gwynne, an American writer who founded a monthly magazine of the same name in 1920s' Paris. The Boulevardier is essentially the bourbon cousin to the Negroni, though the whiskey gives the drink a different, fascinating character.

Serves 1

30ml (1fl oz) bourbon

30ml (1fl oz) Campari

30ml (1fl oz) sweet vermouth

5cm (2 inch) strip of orange peel, to garnish

Add all the ingredients to a mixing glass, fill with ice and stir for about 20 seconds. Strain into a rocks glass over a large ice cube.

Twist or pinch the orange peel over the glass to express the oils, then drop the peel into the drink and serve.

The Improved Whiskey Cocktail

The Improved Whiskey Cocktail made its print debut in 1862, in *Jerry Thomas' Bar-Tenders Guide*, as an updated version of the Old Fashioned Whiskey Cocktail. The second half of the 19th century gave birth to many of the classic drinks we enjoy today – an explosion of creative mixology that some attribute to an increased array of vermouths, fortified wines, liqueurs and bitters available in the United States at that time.

Serves 1

1 sugar cube

1 teaspoon maraschino liqueur

dash of Angostura bitters

dash of Peychaud's bitters

dash of absinthe

60ml (2fl oz) bourbon

5cm (2 inch) of lemon or orange peel, to garnish

Put the sugar cube in the bottom of a rocks glass, add the maraschino, bitters and absinthe and muddle together.

Add the bourbon and stir until the sugar is completely dissolved.

Add some ice cubes and stir again until well chilled. Twist or pinch the orange or lemon peel over the glass to express the oils, then drop the peel into the drink and serve.

Old Fashioned

Originally referred to as simply the Whiskey Cocktail, the term Old Fashioned first appeared in print in 1880 and was used to differentiate it from the Improved Whiskey Cocktail developed by famed barman Jerry Thomas. There is much debate about whether the drink should include muddled fruit or a simple citrus peel for garnish; my suggestion is to try it with the citrus peel first before trying the muddled version.

Serves 1

1 sugar cube

3 dashes of Angostura bitters

dash of water or soda water

60ml (2fl oz) bourbon

5cm (2 inch) of orange or lemon peel, to garnish

Put the sugar cube in the bottom of a rocks glass, add the bitters and water or soda water and muddle together. Add the bourbon and stir until the sugar is completely dissolved.

Add some ice cubes and stir again until chilled. Twist or pinch the orange or lemon peel over the glass to express the oils, then drop the peel into the drink and serve.

Bourbon Hot Toddy

The word "toddy" is an Anglicization of a Hindi drink made from the fermented sap of palm trees. By 1786, a toddy was commonly understood to mean a mixture of alcohol, hot water, sugar and spices. At that time, the toddy was praised as a "cure-all" and while any health claim is dubious, the mixture of warm water, honey, lemon, alcohol and spices can certainly make you feel better on a cold night or help soothe a sore throat.

Serves 1

60ml (2fl oz) bourbon

15ml (½fl oz) freshly squeezed

lemon juice 125ml (4fl oz) hot water 1 teaspoon honey

To garnish

lemon wedge

cinnamon stick (optional)

Add all the ingredients to a mug, coffee cup or glass cup with a handle and stir to dissolve the honey.

Garnish with a lemon wedge. For an autumn or winter cocktail, add a cinnamon stick, if liked.

Whiskey Sour

The Whiskey Sour dates back to at least 1870, when one of the first mentions of the drink can be found in an American newspaper. While this drink has survived for the last 150 years, its popularity has waxed and waned at various points, in part because of the widespread use of pre-made sweet-and-sour cocktail mixes. However, this easy recipe, using fresh lemon juice and sugar syrup, creates a bright, refreshing and simple cocktail that is well worth a try.

Serves 1

45ml (1½fl oz) bourbon

20ml (¾fl oz) freshly squeezed

lemon juice

20ml (¾fl oz) Simple Sugar Syrup

To garnish

maraschino cherry

lemon or orange wedge

Combine all the ingredients in a cocktail shaker filled with ice. Shake, then strain into a rocks glass over ice.

Garnish with a maraschino cherry and lemon or orange wedge.

Mint Julep

The Mint Julep is one of the oldest American cocktails and it's still going strong. The Mint Julep is traditionally made with crushed ice and served in a silver cup – both of which were seen as an outward display of wealth and luxury in the 19th century.

Serves 1

2 teaspoons Simple Sugar Syrup

8–10 mint leaves, plus 1 mint sprig to garnish

60–90ml (2–3fl oz) bourbon

Add the syrup and mint leaves to the bottom of a julep cup or Old Fashioned glass. Gently bruise the leaves with a muddler to release their oils but not so much that they break into small pieces.

Fill the cup or glass halfway with crushed ice. Add the bourbon and stir to combine the ingredients.

Top up the cup or glass with crushed ice and stir until the outside appears frosted. Add more crushed ice and garnish with the mint sprig.

Whiskey Smash

The Whiskey Smash is a variation of the classic Mint Julep, which can use whiskey, brandy, gin, tequila or whatever spirit you particularly fancy. We see the Smash appear in both Jerry Thomas' 1887 revised edition and *Harry Johnson's 1888 Bartender's Manual*. Over the years the specifics of how the drink is made have changed – some use crushed ice, some don't – but the basic structure of spirit, mint, sweet and sour have remained the same.

Serves 1

4–6 mint leaves, plus 1 mint sprig to garnish

½ lemon, cut into wedges

60ml (2fl oz) bourbon

20ml (¾fl oz) Simple Sugar Syrup

Gently muddle the mint leaves and lemon wedges in the bottom of a cocktail shaker, then fill with ice. Add the remaining ingredients, shake and double-strain into a rocks glass filled with ice.

Slap the mint sprig to release its aromatics and add to the drink to garnish.

Serve with a short straw.

Manhattan

The best record for the Manhattan's origin indicates that it was invented by a New York bartender named Black in the 1860s. Given the time and location of its origin, the original version probably used rye whiskey – however, bourbon Manhattans are delicious, and are my personal favourite.

Serves 1

60ml (2fl oz) bourbon 30ml (1fl oz) sweet vermouth
dashes of Angostura bitters
maraschino cherry, to garnish

Combine all the ingredients in a mixing glass and add some ice. Stir, then strain into a chilled cocktail glass.

Garnish with a maraschino cherry.

Remember the Maine

This drink was created by Charles H. Baker and published in his 1939 book *The Gentleman's Companion*. The drink is named after the USS Maine, which sank in the harbour at Havana and was one of the sparks that started the Spanish–American War. Baker recalls creating and enjoying the drink in Havana during the 1933 Cuban Revolution. While this is traditionally made with rye whiskey, bourbon also works very well. Cherry Heering liqueur should be available from specialist drinks stores and is essential to this recipe for the additional spices that it contributes.

Serves 1

60ml (2fl oz) bourbon

20ml (¾fl oz) sweet vermouth

2 teaspoons Cherry Heering liqueur

½ teaspoon absinthe

Combine all the ingredients in a mixing glass and add some ice. Stir for about 30 seconds, then strain into a chilled cocktail glass.

Scofflaw

Created in 1924 at Harry's Bar in Paris, the drink was named for those Americans who continued to drink and flout the US Prohibition laws in place back home.

Serves 1

60ml (2fl oz) bourbon

30ml (1fl oz) dry vermouth

1½ teaspoons freshly squeezed lemon juice

15ml (½fl oz) grenadine

2 dashes of orange bitters

Combine all the ingredients in a cocktail shaker filled with ice. Shake, then strain into a chilled cocktail glass.

Bourbon Flip

Flips are a class of cocktails that are frothed. Originally, pokers of red-hot iron were used to stir a mixture of beer, rum and sugar to a frothy head, although keeping a red-hot poker to hand can be problematic. By 1862 the cold flip shows up in *Jerry Thomas' Bar-Tenders Guide*, with the eggs providing a similar frothy texture.

Serves 1

45ml (1½fl oz) bourbon

1 egg

30ml (1fl oz) Simple Sugar Syrup

freshly grated nutmeg, to garnish

Combine all the ingredients in a cocktail shaker with some ice. Shake thoroughly until the egg is completely combined, then strain into a coupe or other stemmed cocktail glass.

Garnish with freshly grated nutmeg.

Derby

Not much is known about the exact history of the Derby except that it is a very popular name for a cocktail. By 1947 there were at least three commonly accepted variations of this drink, each of which was published in the *Bartender's Guide* by Trader Vic. This recipe is known as the sour-style Derby.

Serves 1

30ml (1fl oz) bourbon

20ml (¾fl oz) freshly squeezed lime juice

15ml (½fl oz) sweet vermouth

15ml (½fl oz) Orange Curaçao or Grand Marnier

lime wedge, to garnish

Combine all the ingredients in a cocktail shaker filled with ice. Shake, then strain into a chilled cocktail glass.

Garnish with a lime wedge.

Variation

To make a Manhattan-style Derby, combine 60ml (2fl oz) bourbon, 1½ teaspoons Bénédictine and a dash of Angostura bitters in a mixing glass and add some ice. Stir, strain into a chilled cocktail glass and garnish with a lime wedge.

Bourbon Highball

Adapted from a Scotch and Soda, the Highball became a very popular drink in the late 19th century. The name "Highball" has a much-disputed etymology, but leaving that aside, the drink itself is simple, refreshing and well worth trying.

Serves 1

30ml (1fl oz) bourbon

soda water, to taste

twist of citrus peel or maraschino cherry, to garnish

Fill a tall glass, such as a highball or Collins glass, with ice then pour over the bourbon. Add an equal or greater part of soda water to lengthen the drink and stir. The drink should retain the flavour of the bourbon but be lighter and refreshing.

Finish with a garnish of your choice. Try a twist of citrus peel or a maraschino cherry.

Bourbon Collins

Sometimes referred to as a John Collins, this cocktail and the more widespread Tom Collins are essentially spirited sparkling lemonades. The John Collins first appeared in the *Steward and Barkeeper's Manual* from 1869. The original recipe called for Old Tom gin, which probably explains why the drink's name changed to the Tom Collins in *Jerry Thomas' Bar-Tenders Guide*. the Bourbon Collins is a variation on this theme.

Serves 1

60ml (2fl oz) bourbon

30ml (1fl oz) freshly squeezed lemon juice

20ml (¾fl oz) Simple Sugar Syrup

soda water, to top up

To garnish

orange slice

maraschino cherry

Combine all the ingredients, except the soda water, in a cocktail shaker filled with ice. Shake, then strain into a glass filled with ice.

Top up with soda water, stir and garnish with an orange slice and maraschino cherry.

Bourbon Rickey

A variation of the Bourbon Highball, the Bourbon Rickey was created by George A. Williamson at Shoomaker's in Washington, D.C. in 1883. The drink gets its name from Democratic lobbyist Colonel Joe Rickey, who frequented the bar and enjoyed drinking bourbon and soda on hot D.C. days.

Serves 1

½ lime

45ml (1½fl oz) bourbon

soda water, to top up

Fill a highball glass with ice. Squeeze over the juice from the lime half, then drop the lime into the glass and add the bourbon.

Top up with soda water and give a quick stir to mix the ingredients.

Bourbon Daisy

The Daisy is a type of classic cocktail that was created in the mid-19th century. In the *Bar-Tenders Guide*, Jerry Thomas includes versions of the Daisy that can be made with brandy, gin and – as here – whiskey.

Serves 1

60ml (2fl oz) bourbon

30ml (1fl oz) freshly squeezed lemon juice

1½ teaspoons grenadine

1½ teaspoons Simple Sugar Syrup

tonic water, to top up

To garnish

orange slice

maraschino cherry

Combine all the ingredients except the tonic water in a cocktail shaker filled with ice. Shake for about 20 seconds, then pour into a glass over ice.

Top up with tonic water, stir once and garnish with an orange slice and maraschino cherry.

Bourbon Lift

While this is not a classic cocktail in terms of its age, its creator, Jennifer Colliau, combined two classic drinks – the Fizz and the New York Egg Cream – into something very original. The drink was adapted by Erik Adkins of the Slanted Door Group, and here calls for bourbon – and not brandy – as its base spirit.

Serves 1

45ml (1½fl oz) bourbon
15ml (½fl oz) double cream (heavy cream)
15ml (½fl oz) coffee liqueur
15ml (½fl oz) almond orgeat
soda water, to top up

Combine all the ingredients, except the soda water, in a cocktail shaker filled with ice. Shake for about 10 seconds, then double-strain into a Collins glass.

From about 15cm (6 inches) above the rim of the glass, pour soda water into the drink until the foam begins to bloom over the edge. Wait for a few seconds and then add a little more soda water to lift the head higher above the rim. Serve with a straw.

Bourbon and Ginger Punch

While it is common to see whiskey and cola, or whiskey and ginger ale, prepared and served as an individual cocktail, the simplicity and mass appeal of a bourbon and ginger punch make it an easy crowd-pleaser to make in larger quantities.

Serves 1

1 part bourbon

2½ parts ginger ale

orange wheels, to garnish

Combine the bourbon and ginger ale in a large punch bowl, then garnish with orange wheels on the surface of the punch.

The punch can be chilled by either serving it over ice in small cups or glasses, or placing a large block of ice in the punch bowl.

Bourbon Apple Punch

While this particular recipe cannot be called a classic, the flavour that it produces certainly can, combining bourbon with apple, honey and baking spices. Freshly grated nutmeg will give a stronger flavour than ground.

Serves 6

90ml (3fl oz) lemon juice

85g (3oz) honey

¼ teaspoon ground cinnamon

¼ teaspoon freshly grated or ground nutmeg

225ml (8fl oz) bourbon

350ml (12fl oz) unfiltered (cloudy) apple juice

8 dashes of Angostura bitters

225ml (8fl oz) soda water

To garnish

apple slices

rosemary sprig

Mix together the lemon juice, honey, cinnamon and nutmeg until well blended. Pour into a punch bowl, then stir in the bourbon, apple juice and bitters.

Top up with the soda water and garnish with apple slices and a sprig of rosemary.

Bourbon Eggnog

Eggnog is a very popular drink with an uncertain origin and etymology. However, we do know that a drink called "eggnog" containing eggs, dairy, alcohol and sugar shows up in the American colonies around the mid-1700s. George Washington was known to serve eggnog to visitors, using a recipe that included a mix of brandy, rye whiskey, rum and sherry. Homemade eggnog can be made with any alcohol, and bourbon does a particularly nice job, especially if you use a variety that leans toward the fruity or vanilla end of the flavour spectrum.

Serves 8

6 eggs

200g (7oz) granulated sugar

½ teaspoon salt

250ml (9fl oz) bourbon

1 teaspoon vanilla extract

1 litre (2 pints) single cream (light cream)

freshly grated nutmeg, to garnish

In a large bowl, whisk the eggs until frothy. Add the sugar and salt and continue to whisk until the sugar is dissolved. Stir in the remaining ingredients.

Chill for at least 3 hours. Serve garnished with a sprinkling of nutmeg.

Bourbon

How to read the label

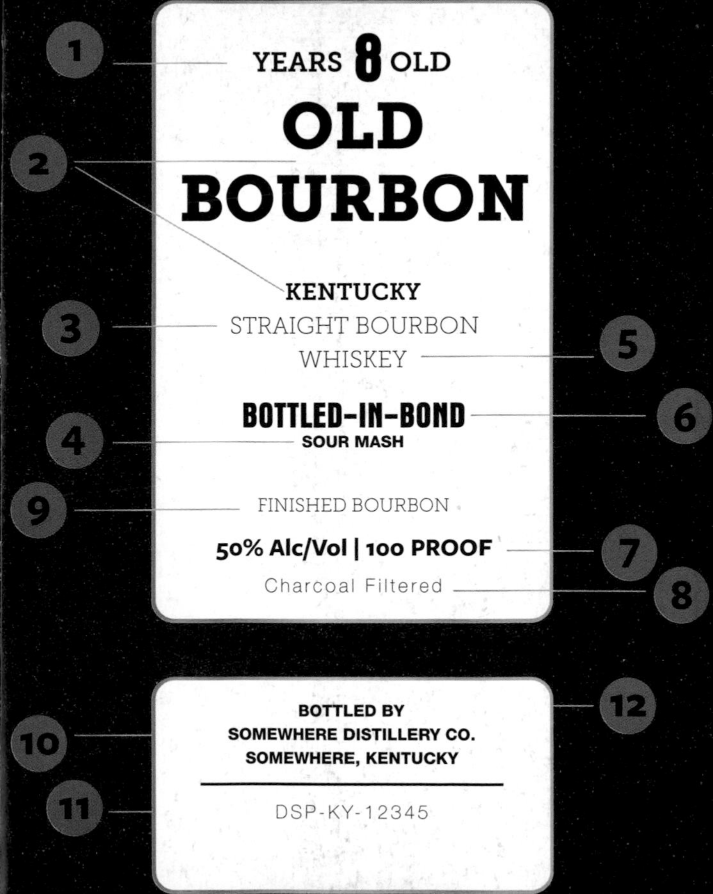

YEARS **8** OLD

OLD
BOURBON

KENTUCKY
STRAIGHT BOURBON
WHISKEY

BOTTLED-IN-BOND
SOUR MASH

FINISHED BOURBON

50% Alc/Vol | 100 PROOF
Charcoal Filtered

BOTTLED BY
SOMEWHERE DISTILLERY CO.
SOMEWHERE, KENTUCKY

DSP-KY-12345

When you pick up a bottle of bourbon, the label provides a lot of information about the liquid contained inside – especially if you know what to look for. This information can be traced back to the very first consumer protection legislation passed by the US Congress in 1897 – the Bottled-in-Bond Act. The Act served as the basis from which all other US alcohol labelling laws sprung and these laws help to inform consumers about what they are buying simply by reading the label.

Now, it is also true that the label may not tell you everything you want to know, or in some cases may be slightly misleading – which is why it is important to know how to read a bourbon label and understand what is and what is not being said.

1 Age Statements By US law, bourbon is required to have an age statement for the youngest bourbon in the bottle on the front, back, side or neck label. However, there is an exception to this rule. If a bourbon is labelled as straight or bottled-in-bond and is aged for at least four years, the producer has the option of not adding an additional age statement on the label. This is why there are no specific age statements listed on Jim Beam White Label, Evan Williams Black Label, Wild Turkey 101 and many other straight bourbons from Kentucky. One recent trend seen mostly on craft bourbons and bourbons from non-distilling producers (NDPs) has been the use of "Aged less than 4 years". Labels featuring this are an unfortunate development, because they do not conform to either the letter or the spirit of the law. The purpose of requiring an age statement is to allow consumers to make an informed decision when making their purchase. Saying something is less than four years old isn't as clear as it could be – is it six months old? Or three years? Producers who use this statement on their labels might be making fine bourbon, but they are not being completely transparent.

2 Brand Name An obvious inclusion, you will probably find this on the bottle in some shape or form. The brand name is also sometimes known as the fanciful name. **State of Distillation** It is required by US law that all bourbon bottles specify the state in which the whiskey was distilled, and this information can be found in a few places on the bottle. It is usually specified quite clearly on the front, but some bourbon producers – particularly those outside of Kentucky – choose instead to put the state of distillation on the back. Taking Jim Beam as an example, you'll see the state once on the front label identifying that the straight bourbon is from the state of Kentucky and again on the back label, with an address. If the bourbon is distilled in one state and bottled in a second state, the label must say "Distilled in…" separately from the bottling address on the label.

③ Straight This is a US Alcohol and Tobacco Tax and Trade Bureau's (TTB) legally defined term and means a whiskey stored in a charred new oak container for at least two years and to which no colouring, flavouring or blending materials are added, other than water. Without this term, bourbon is allowed to have added harmless colouring, flavouring or blending materials that do not alter the class of the spirit – similar to Scotch whisky, which can have a colouring agent known as E150a added without the need for it to be specified on the label. **Blended Bourbon** "A blend" is a legally defined term, specifying whiskey that must contain at least 51% straight bourbon blended with other whiskey and/or a neutral spirit such as high-proof vodka. Blended bourbon may also contain harmless colouring, flavouring or blending materials. **Blended Straight Bourbon Whiskeys** "Blended" or "a blend of" straight bourbon whiskeys is legally defined by the TTB as a mixture of straight bourbon whiskeys that come from more than one producer in one or more states. These blends are also allowed to contain harmless colouring, flavouring or blending materials. If the mixture includes straight bourbons from two or more states, then the producer is not required to put the state of distillation on the label. Most examples of blended straight bourbon whiskeys on the market today are this sort of mixture, combining bourbons from more than one state.

4 **Sour Mash** This is an unregulated term that can refer to two different production techniques that aid in the fermentation of a bourbon mash. One method takes a portion of a fermented mash that is full of live yeast and pitches it into a new unfermented batch of grain. This inoculates the new mash with some active yeast and lowers the pH level of the mash, making it more acidic, which is good for the yeast and bad for other bacteria that could cause the mash to spoil. A second method sometimes referred to as a sour mash is when spent beer is added to a new batch of fermenting grain. While the spent beer does not have any live yeast, it does have a low pH level, which helps the fresh yeast in the new mash outcompete any bacteria or other microorganisms.

5 **Whiskey** Whiskey is a general class of spirit – and, as the saying goes, all bourbons are whiskey but not all whiskeys are bourbon. The TTB defines whiskey as an alcoholic distillate made from a fermented mash of grain distilled to less than 95% alcohol by volume (ABV) in such a way that it "possesses the taste, aroma and characteristics generally attributed to whiskey", stored in oak barrels and bottled at a minimum of 40% ABV. Interestingly, even though whiskey spelt with an "e" is the most common spelling in the United States, the TTB spells whisky without an "e" in all of its rules – with "whiskey" to be used on labels as an allowable alternative spelling. What this means in practice is that most bourbon producers choose to spell whiskey with an "e", although a few brands such as Maker's Mark have adopted the spelling (without an "e") more common to the rest of the world. **Bourbon** "Bourbon" is a TTB legally defined term, meaning a whiskey made from a fermented mash of grains – with no less than 51% corn – distilled to no more than 80% ABV and stored at no more than 62.5% ABV in a charred new oak container. In addition to corn, the typical grains found in bourbon are rye, wheat and malted barley, although any grain could be included. What you might notice is absent from the definition of bourbon is a statement about where it is made and how long the bourbon must stay in the barrel. The reasons are simple. First, bourbon can be made anywhere in the United States, not just Kentucky. Second, there is no legally mandated length of time a bourbon must stay in the charred new oak barrel unless it is modified with the term straight or bottled-in-bond. This means a bourbon could be stored in the barrel for as long as it takes to fill it up and then immediately be dumped. In practice, of course, almost no one does this and the vast majority of bourbon consumed around the world is at least four years old. **Tennessee Whiskey** Since the signing of the North

American Free Trade Agreement in 1992, all US trade agreements have included protection for Tennessee whiskey as a straight bourbon whiskey distinctive to the State of Tennessee. In May 2013, Tennessee went a step further and created a state law that officially defined Tennessee whiskey as: a spirit manufactured in Tennessee; filtered through maple charcoal prior to ageing, also known as the Lincoln County Process; made from grain that consists of at least 51% corn; distilled to no more than 160 proof (80% ABV); aged in charred new oak barrels; placed in the barrel at no more than 125 proof (62.5% ABV); and bottled at not less than 80 proof (40% ABV). The last five parts of this definition exactly mirror the TTB's legal definition for bourbon, which means Tennessee whiskey is bourbon, but most Tennessee whiskey producers choose not to label it as bourbon – presumably for marketing reasons.

6 Small Batch "Small batch" is an unregulated term invented by Kentucky bourbon distillers to distinguish certain bourbons in their portfolio from the rest. As the term is not legally outlined there is no singular definition. Generally, it has come to mean that the bourbon in the bottle comes from a small number of barrels (often 50–200), compared to the thousands of barrels used for a single bottling run of a large brand. "Small batch" is pure marketing-speak and is almost impossible to quantify in terms of actual value for the consumer. Despite this vagueness, the term has caught on since Heaven Hill first released its Elijah Craig Small Batch Bourbon in 1986, and countless producers both big and small have used it as a justification for a higher price point. **Single Barrel** "Single barrel" is another term that is not legally defined by the TTB – however, it does require all labels to be truthful, so the plain meaning of the term is self-evident and refers to the fact that all of the whiskey in the bottle came from one barrel. It is common on single barrel bourbon labels to see the producer list the barrel number that the bottle was filled from. **Bottled-in-Bond** This is a legally defined term for a whiskey that has been aged for at least four years in charred new oak containers, the product of one single distillery, from one single distilling season and bottled at exactly 100 proof (50% ABV). This was once the gold standard for bourbon and a true sign of quality, but bottled-in-bond bourbons slowly fell out of favour as bourbon producers chased the changing tastes of drinkers in the 1970s and 1980s toward lighter flavoured spirits. However, both the large Kentucky distilleries and a growing number of craft distillers are offering bottled-in-bond bourbon once again as a product of quality and authenticity. **Craft** The word craft when it comes to distilled spirits is a completely unregulated term by the TTB. However, there are a few organizations that have created definitions to help bring clarity. The most universally accepted aspect of what defines a craft distillery or a craft spirit is production size. While this can range from 30,000–750,000 proof gallons, depending on the organization, the main idea is that craft spirits come from distilleries that have significantly smaller total capacity compared to Jim Beam, for example, which in 2016 sold about 9 million proof gallons. A proof gallon is 1 gallon of spirit at 50% ABV. The American Distilling Institute and the American Craft Spirits Association both add an additional condition that craft spirits come from distilleries which are independently owned, not owned by a conglomerate of spirit brands or a multinational corporation. Aware of the large market share they have lost to craft brewers; large spirit brands have begun using craft language in their marketing materials in an attempt to cash in on the interest in craft spirits and slow any potential loss of market share.

7 Alcohol Concentration US law requires all bourbons to disclose the concentration of alcohol in the spirit by volume, expressed as a percentage. Many bourbons are around the 40% ABV mark, which is the lowest legally allowable ABV for a bourbon to be bottled at in the United States. However, outside the US it is possible to find examples of bourbon bottled at less than 40% ABV. The TTB also allows producers the option to include the alcohol concentration expressed in US proof, which is simply two times the ABV – so a 40% ABV bourbon is 80 proof.

Cask Strength/Barrel Proof "Cask strength" and "barrel proof" are not legally defined terms, but they refer to the fact that the bourbon in the bottle has not been diluted with water to reduce its strength. This does not mean that the bourbon has not been filtered. It is still possible that the spirit was lightly filtered to remove any charcoal sediment from the barrel or it was chill filtered to remove excess fatty acids that can cause a spirit to become cloudy.

8 **Non Chill Filtered** Chill filtering is a process by which bourbon is cooled down to a temperature between -10°C (14°F) and 4°C (39°F), then filtered through paper to remove any long-chain fatty acids. These fatty acids are not dangerous in any way but they can cause a spirit to look cloudy and less attractive, so this is done mostly for aesthetic reasons. However, some producers claim that these fatty acids contribute to the flavour and mouthfeel of the spirit, so will proudly state that their bourbons are not chill filtered. **Charcoal Filtered** Charcoal filtration is a process in which the bourbon passes through a charcoal medium to remove any sediment from the barrel or larger particles. It has been incorrectly claimed by some that the reason Tennessee whiskey is not labelled as bourbon is because it goes through what is known as the Lincoln

County Process, in which the new spirit is charcoal filtered before going into a barrel. Charcoal filtration does not prohibit a company in any way from labelling its whiskey as a bourbon.

9 **Finished Bourbon** Finished bourbon describes a process where the whiskey is dumped from its original charred new oak barrel and transferred to a second barrel that previously contained another liquid, such as beer, wine, sherry, port, rum, brandy, maple syrup or even roasted coffee beans. This second maturation is usually over a much shorter period, but allows the bourbon to pick up additional flavours before it is vatted, proofed and bottled.

10 **Address for Production** It is a requirement of US law to include the state in which the whiskey was distilled and bottled. The industry norm is just to list the city and state but there are loopholes in this process that can actually obscure where and who made the bourbon in the bottle. Producers are permitted to use a different business name, also known as a DBA (Doing Business As), meaning a larger company can subcontract a distillery to create its bourbon and hide the name of either from the bottle – giving an impression of a more local, small-scale production. This marketing sleight of hand simply means that you need to take this information with a pinch of salt.

11 DSP Number A Distilled Spirits Producer (DSP) number is assigned to a facility when it receives its US federal permit to operate a distillery, or some other business that handles or bottles distilled spirits, and includes the state along with a specific number. For example, Jim Beam operates DSP-KY-230, which is a distillery in Clermont, Kentucky. At present, including the DSP number on a label is optional, although some have suggested that if this became mandatory it could help consumers to make informed decisions about their purchases and provide greater transparency.

12 Production Statements TTB requires all bourbon labels to say "Bottled by" followed by the company that put the bourbon into the bottle. This can be modified to: "Produced and bottled by", "Made by", "Handmade", "Crafted" and "Handcrafted" etc. None of these, however, necessarily mean that the company actually fermented, distilled, aged and bottled the bourbon, only that the company took bourbon barrels and bottled the contents. If you are interested in drinking whiskey actually made by a particular distillery, look for the words "Distilled and bottled by" – some have gone a step further to include "Fermented, distilled, aged and bottled by" on the label.

GLOSSARY

ABV: Alcohol by Volume.

Angel's share: The portion of spirit, both alcohol and water, that evaporates from wooden barrels each year. The angel's share varies based on temperature, humidity and atmospheric pressure.

Backset: A portion of fully fermented mash held back and used to create a sour mash in a new fermentation.

Blending: When used as a legal term on a TTB-approved label in the US, this refers to the addition of neutral spirit and/or harmless blending materials, such as caramel colouring or flavouring.

Bourbon: An American whiskey made primarily from corn and aged in charred new oak barrels. The whiskey cannot be distilled above 80% ABV and must go into the barrel at less than 62.5% ABV.

Cask strength/Barrel proof: Spirit bottled without the addition of water to bring down its strength.

Column distilled: A spirit made using a column still.

Distiller's beer: Fermented mash, added to the still. Dumped: This refers to when the contents of a barrel are emptied before further processing.

Fusel alcohols: From the German for "bad liquor", these are higher-order alcohols formed during fermentation at high temperatures, low pH or when yeast activity is limited by a lack of nitrogen. In spirits, high concentrations of fusel

alcohols can produce off flavours and create a hot or harsh sensation in the mouth.

Grist: The ground-up grain solids of a mash.

Heads: The volatile and toxic compounds such as methanol and acetone that are removed from the spirit before most of the ethanol begins to volatilize.

Hearts: The centre cut of the spirit that comes off the still. This consists primarily of ethanol, water and pleasant flavour compounds.

Lincoln County Process: A required process for most Tennessee whiskey. New-make spirit is first filtered through a column of sugar maple charcoal before going into a charred new oak barrel.

Low wines: The spirit collected after the first run of a pot still. The low wines are collected and then put into the still for a second spirit run.

Mash: The mixture of grain that is cooked and fermented before being distilled.

Mash bill: The ratio of grains specific for a style of whiskey. In the case of bourbon the mash bill must consist of at least 51% corn with the other 49% from other grains.

Master Distiller: A title bestowed on a distiller who has accumulated decades of experience and knowledge producing spirits. This term is sometimes misappropriated by less experienced distillers who happen to be the more senior distiller at their company.

Neat: An unmixed spirit served without water, ice or a mixer.

New-make spirit: Newly distilled spirit that is ready to go into a barrel to mature into whiskey.

Pot distilled: A spirit produced on a pot still.

Proof: In the US proof is simply double the ABV. In the UK, 100 proof was assigned as the alcoholic strength at which gun powder, wetted with alcohol, would ignite, which is just above 57% ABV.

Proofing: The process of bringing down a spirit's alcohol concentration, usually with the addition of water or lower-strength spirit.

Pulled: When a barrel is removed from the rickhouse after reaching maturity.

Single barrel bourbon: Bourbon that has been bottled completely from one barrel.

Small batch bourbon: An unregulated term created by Kentucky distilleries. It usually refers to a whiskey that comes from the vatting of a small number of barrels (50–200 is often cited) as opposed to many hundreds or even thousands of barrels vatted for a single bottling run of one of the larger Kentucky bourbons.

Sour mash: A mash that has had its pH lowered with the addition of backset, stillage or spent beer. This makes the mash more acidic (sour) which helps the yeast to outcompete other microorganisms that might spoil the mash.

Spent beer: The remaining liquid with some residual solids after the alcohol has been stripped out.

Stillage: The leftover liquid and some solids from a distillation run.

Straight: Used to describe whiskey that has been aged for at least two years in charred new oak barrels.

Tails: The heavier fusel alcohols that come off the still after the hearts. The tails are sometimes collected and added to a striping run to extract a little extra alcohol.

TTB: US Alcohol and Tobacco Tax and Trade Bureau.

Vatting: The process of mixing (blending) spirits or barrels of spirits together.

Whiskey: An aged grain spirit. In the US there is no minimum amount of time whiskey must stay in a barrel before it can be called whiskey, however it must go into a barrel for some amount of time and in practice, the vast majority of American whiskey is at least four years old.

Whisky/whiskey: The spelling most frequently used in the US is with an "e", while the spelling without an "e" is most commonly used in the rest of the world. The TTB actually spells "whisky" without an "e" but allows the spelling with an "e" to be used as an alternate spelling on labels. Now, as to why there are two spellings for whiskey, and why the US has favoured one more than the other, this is a complicated story best described in a series of blog posts titled "Whiskey vs Whisky" on www.Ezdrinking.com.

White dog: A name given to new-make spirit, before it is aged. Sometimes white dog is also described as moonshine.

CONVERSIONS

UK	US
Autumn	Fall
Banoffee	Mixture of banana and toffee sauce
Cherry Bakewell	An open tart shell coated with a layer of preserves and filled with an almond-flavoured sponge cake.
Desiccated coconut	Dry coconut
Double cream	Heavy cream
Mixed spice	Allspice
Single cream	Light cream
Soda water	Club soda
Spirit	Liquor
Sticky toffee pudding	A sponge cake with dates and covered in a toffee sauce
Top up	Top off
Treacle	Molasses
Unfiltered (cloudy) apple juice	Apple cider (sweet)